I0558477

THE BOOKLET ON
HOW ONE BECOMES
BORN AGAIN
OR SAVED THROUGH
JESUS CHRIST

REV. DR. SANDRA Y. WASHINGTON

DENISE M. JOHNSON, EDITOR

Copyright © 2024 by Rev. Dr. Sandra Y. Washington.

ISBN: 979-8-89465-004-3 (sc)
ISBN: 979-8-89465-005-0 (e)

All rights reserved. No part of this publication may be reproduced,
distributed, or transmitted in any form or by any means, including
photocopying, recording, or other electronic or mechanical methods,
without the prior written permission of the author, except in the case
of brief quotations embodied in critical reviews and certain other
noncommercial uses permitted by copyright law.

Printed in the United States of America.

Integrity Publishing
39343 Harbor Hills Blvd Lady Lake,
FL 32159

www.integrity-publishing.com

TABLE OF CONTENTS

ACKNOWLEDGEMENT

Many thanks to my Lord, Jesus Christ who has inspired me to write a booklet on "How One Becomes Born Again or Saved Through Jesus Christ". It took me awhile to get started to write this booklet. Many thanks to Pastor James Varlack Jr. of Greater Love Ministries of Our Lord Jesus Christ, Inc. and The Church of the First Born, Inc., in Queens, N.Y., where I serve as a musician and member of the Church. He encouraged me to write a book concerning receiving Salvation for the Blind. I informed him that God has already inspired me to write a book concerning the process of being born again. He said that was great!! Apostle Varlack suggested that I contact his friend, Pastor Barry Carver, who ministers preaching at his church called, "Organic Gospel Hour"

I thanked both of the pastors for inspiring me to write a booklet on the process of being born again that was already within my spirit to write, but I did not realize so soon that writing the book would serve as an evangelistic tool for blind people and for all readers. However, apparently, God wanted me to get started writing the book through the encouragement of Pastor Varlack Jr. and Pastor Barry Carver. Again, many thanks to both of them.

INTRODUCTION

In this booklet, one would learn the process of how a sinner is born again in his human spirit that is dormant. He has no connection with God unless it is by the Holy Spirit, through the acceptance of Jesus Christ's Spirit. However, this booklet will teach steps on how one can connect to the one and only true God by accepting the person of Jesus Christ and His Spirit. The readers will learn about the purposes and deeds of the person of the Holy Spirit and His ability to start the salvation process - changing the human spirit from a dormant state into God's divine nature of having eternal life. Would you accept Christ today in your heart?

TOPIC: THE PROCESS OF BEING BORN AGAIN INTO THE KINGDOM OF GOD

CHAPTER 1

BEING BORN AGAIN

A – Introduction Statement: When we were unbelievers, our human spirits were dormant or asleep in spiritual darkness with the sin nature consciousness. This caused spiritual blindness and separation from God's Spirit and Presence.

B - Defining "Born Again": According to Jesus Christ's definition of Being born again is in John 3:5-6 (NLT), He said to Nicodemus, the Pharisee, "I assure you no one can enter the Kingdom of God without being born of water and the Spirit. Humans can reproduce only human life, but the Holy Spirit gives birth to spiritual life."

In other words, being born again is the Rebirthing of our human Spirit by the Holy Spirit of God. The Spirit of God regenerates or transitions our human spirit from darkness of the sin nature of Satan's kingdom into having God's divine nature and light in order to enter God's Kingdom.

C - The purpose of Being Born Again:

1. To be in communion and communication with the whole Godhead spiritually. Colossian 2:9-10 and 1Cor. 13:14
2. To be born into the Kingdom of God as children of God, Romans 8:16
3. To be born as heirs and joint heirs with Jesus Christ, Romans 8:17; what belongs to Jesus in His Kingdom He has given to us as born again believers John 16:15.

We can say then that being born again is a wonderful spiritual experience as our spiritual eyes and human spirit are awakened by the Spirit of God to being in one spirit with God through the Holy Spirit of Jesus Christ.

In Chapter 2, I will discuss how an unbeliever can be born again.

CHAPTER 2

HOW TO BE BORN AGAIN

A - A diagram of a black candle with a wick – represents the unbeliever whose human spirit is dormant in the conscious darkness of sin nature; spiritually blind and separate from God's Spirit.

"Candle represents a Sinner"

"The sinner has no connection with God's Spirit."  "The sinner's human spirit is with the sin nature."

B - After the unbeliever hears a Salvation message presented by the testimony of a minister of Christ, the invitation to receive Jesus Christ is offered. The unbeliever accepts Jesus Christ in his or her heart, saying a sinner's prayer based on Romans 10:9-10 (Read)

C - What has the unbeliever become after receiving Jesus Christ?

"This candle represents
the sinner becoming a born again saint"

"The saint's body is  "The saint has God's
the temple of God's Spirit in his human
Spirit." spirit."

We, Christians who were once unbelievers have accepted Jesus Christ as our personal savior, the Holy Spirit instantly enters our human spirit to redeem it and rebirth it from the darkness of:

1. the sin nature generated by the Holy Spirit into the divine nature and light of God as we enter His Kingdom forever, Titus 3:4-5

2. We are no longer sinners but saints; you can't be both. You're either a sinner without Christ's Spirit or a Saint with Christ's Spirit. Ephesians 2: 8,9 (NLT) Paul says by the Holy Spirit, "God saved you by His grace when you believed. And you can't take credit for this, it is a gift from God. Salvation is not a reward for the good things we have done, so none of us can boast about it. In 1John 3:9 (NLT) The Apostle John says to the believers,

Those who have been born into God's family does not make a practice of sinning because God's life is in them. So they can't keep on sinning because they are the born of God.

We have become a new man spiritually. Old habits have no more control; behold new things of God has begun in you spiritually, 2Cor 5:17. We have the law of love within us stated by Jesus Christ when He walked the earth saying in Matthew 22:37-40 (NLT), "You must love the Lord your God with all your heart, all your soul and all your mind. This is the first and greatest commandment. A second is equally important: love your neighbor as yourself. The entire law and all the demands of the Prophets are based on these two commandments."

3. You and I have become temples of the Holy Spirit who is the living God within us, 1Cor. 6:19. Therefore we have the eternal life because of the Eternal Spirit within us, Hebrews 9:14.

4. We have become righteous, a holy nation, a royal priesthood, a peculiar people 1 Peter 2:9.

Therefore, if we are the temples of the living God, the very presence of God lives in us. In my next chapters 3 will deal with the purpose of having the Holy Spirit within Christians.

CHAPTER 3

THE PURPOSES OF HAVING THE HOLY SPIRIT WITHIN YOU

A - The Significance Of Having The Holy Spirit

1. To determine our Eternal Life in God's Kingdom through Jesus Christ. Since the Holy Spirit is the third person of the Godhead, He is called the Eternal Spirit, Hebrews 9:14 and John 3:16. Another name for Eternal Life is Everlasting Life.

2. At Salvation, the Holy Spirit regenerates our human spirit from the sin nature to having God's divine nature, Titus 3:4-5.

3. He is the very presence of God within us connecting us to the communion and fellowship of the whole Godhead, Colossian 2:9-10 and Psalm 139:7.

4. The Holy Spirit is responsible for establishing the 9 fruits of the Spirit of God and Jesus Christ which is His character within us Gal.5:22-23.

5. The Holy Spirit is the very voice of God in that He communicates within our human spirit inwardly and outwardly in various ways as He guides us, helps us to do the works of Christ as our Helper or Comforter, reveals to us what is to come, and teaches us through the revelation knowledge of Christ. John 14:16 & John 16:13.

6. The Holy Spirit helps us to live out our Salvation in the strength, power and leading of Christ's Spirit. Philippians 2:12- 13; Gal. 2:20.

7. The Holy Spirit determines our ability to glorify Jesus Christ. John 16:14.

8. He determines within our spirit that we are children of God. Rom. 8:16.

As we can see, the Holy Spirit is very significant to have within us. The good part about Him is that He gets to live within us forever and ever - guiding us, teaching us through revelation knowledge, comforting us, giving us words of wisdom on how to get out of a problem, and showing us things to come concerning our lives.

In Chapter 4 we will talk about the Deity and Deeds of the Holy Spirit.

CHAPTER 4

THE DEITY AND DEEDS OF THE HOLY SPIRIT

A. **THE DEITY OF THE HOLY SPIRIT:** The Holy Spirit is the third person of the Trinity of the whole Godhead, The Father, God, The Son, Jesus Christ and God's Spirit, the Holy Spirit. In short we can say that the Godhead includes God the Father, God the Son and God the Holy Spirit. The three persons in one makes up the Trinity even though the word "Trinity" is not written in the Bible. The three persons include the Father, who is a Spirit, Then His Spirit was embodied in a physical body of Jesus Christ who became God's mouthpiece and God's Spirit, who is the Holy Spirit who determines the manifestation of His Word spoken through His Son, Jesus Christ. He is also the Power and Voice of God who spoke the creation of the earth, the heavens, the planets and humanity into existence caused by the Holy Spirit.

1. **ˑ¹THE HOLY SPIRIT IS OMNIPRESENT:** The Holy Spirit is everywhere at once. Therefore, God and Jesus Christ is everywhere at once. The Holy Spirit is God 1Corinthians 2:11. He is the I AM of God and of Jesus Christ. God is the self-existed one. He is in all and above all.

2. **ˑ²THE HOLY SPIRIT IS OMNIPOTENT:** The Holy Spirit is all powerful God. He is the power of the Most High God. Luke 1:35

3. **ˑ³THE HOLY SPIRIT IS OMNISCIENT:** The Holy Spirit is all knowing for He knows the mind of God. 1Corinthians 2:11. Jesus Christ knew all things by the Holy Spirit. John 21:17.

4. **ˑ⁴THE HOLY SPIRIT GIVES US LIFE:** Through Jesus Christ, the Holy Spirit gives life. Romans 8:2.

5. **ˑ⁵ THE HOLY SPIRIT IS THE ETERNAL SPIRIT:** The Holy Spirit is the Eternal Spirit through whom Jesus Christ offered Himself to God. Hebrews 9:14 In other words, by the Eternal Spirit, Christ offered Himself to God as an atonement for the sins of humanity to fulfil the Law of Sin and Death on behalf of mankind. John 3:16-17 says (NLT), "For God loved the world so much that He gave His one and only Son, so that, everyone who believes in Him, shall not

perish, but have eternal life. God sent His Son not to judge the world but to save the world through Him."

Footnotes with* from 1-5 are taken from reference book, "Rose Book of Bible Charts, Maps and Time Lines" page 39; Topic: "The Holy Spirit And The Names of God".

B – THE DEEDS OF THE HOLY SPIRIT

Some of the deeds of the Holy Spirit operating within Christians are as follows, as stated in John chapter 14:16-17 (NLT), when Jesus said to His disciples and is saying to Christians today: 1. The Holy Spirit is an Advocate or the One that Comforts and walks alongside you. 2. The Holy Spirit will never leave you, 3. The Holy Spirit will lead you into all truth. 4. The Holy Spirit will be with you and will live in you. 5. The Holy Spirit will teach you everything and remind you of everything Jesus has told you.

In relation to the world of unbelievers stated in John 16:8-11 (NLT) proclaimed by Jesus Christ: 6. The Holy Spirit will convict the world of its sin; and of God's righteousness and of the coming Judgment. The world's sin is that it refuses to believe in Me (Jesus); Righteousness is available because I go to the Father, but you will see Me no more; Judgment will come because the ruler of this world has been already judged.

However, Jesus Christ reassures His disciples and us Christians today in John 16:13-18 (NLT) that 7. The Holy Spirit, the Spirit of Truth will guide us in all truth; He will not speak on

His own, but will tell you what He has heard (from God and Jesus Christ); 8. He will tell you about the future (or things to come); 9. The Holy Spirit will bring Me glory by telling you whatever He receives from Me. All that belongs to God is Mine; that is why I said, "The Spirit will tell you whatever He receives from Me".

Paul says to Christians in Galatians 5:22-23 (NLT), 10. "The Holy Spirit produces this kind of fruit in our lives: love, joy, peace, patience (or longsuffering), kindness, goodness, faithfulness, gentleness, and self-control. There is no law against these things." Paul says to the Christians in Romans 8:9-17 (NLT) 11. "But you are not controlled by your sinful nature. You are controlled by the Holy Spirit if you have the Spirit of God living in you. So that by the Holy Spirit, Christ lives within you though your body will die because of sin, the Holy Spirit gives you life; because you have been made right with God." 12. Verse 26 says, "All who are led by the Spirit of God are children of God. 13. The Holy Spirit helps in our weakness when we don't know what to pray for. He prays for us (through us) with groanings…." In Chapter 6 we will discuss communing with the Holy Spirit.

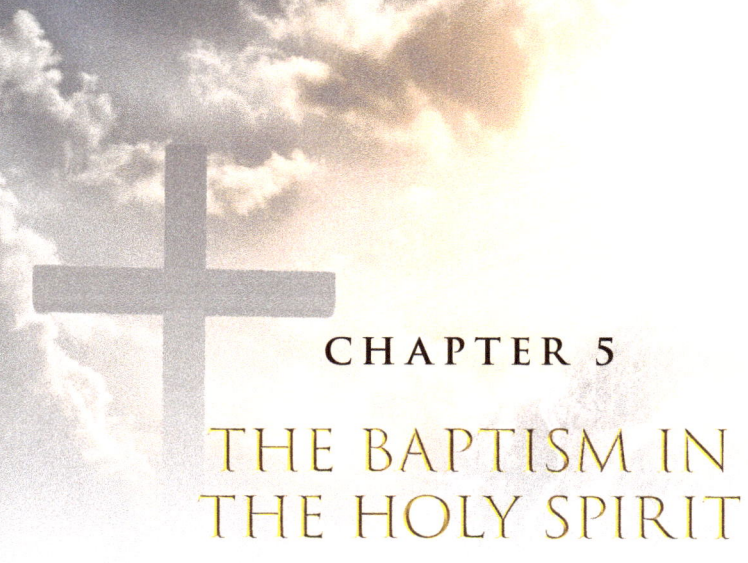

CHAPTER 5

THE BAPTISM IN THE HOLY SPIRIT

A – How To Receive The Baptism In The Holy Spirit Or The Gift of the Holy Spirit.

1. Use of the water demonstration representing the Holy Spirit – a glass of water filled half way is used. The glass represents the believer: (A congregant is selected to demonstrate with water)

    a. As the water is being poured slowly in the glass the speaker says, "At salvation we had received the Holy Spirit when we accepted Jesus Christ as our personal Savior. Therefore, by the Holy Spirit

        1. We were baptized into the family of God as children of God in His Kingdom

        2. We became the temple of the whole Godhead

3. Since the Holy Spirit lives within our human spirit, we are Holy, Righteous and we have the 9 Fruits of the Spirit as the Character of God within us.

4. We have the authority of using Jesus' name when we pray

5. We can communicate with God and God with us.

2. But then there is a second experience, that is, being baptized in the Holy Spirit. Luke 11:13 says, if you can give good gifts to your children, how much more will your heavenly Father give the Holy Spirit to those who ASK Him?"

3. John the Baptist said in Matt. 3:11, he baptized with water, but the one coming after him, He (or Jesus) will baptize us with the Holy Spirit and with Fire".

4. When we ask Jesus to baptize us with the Holy Spirit and with fire our spirit is flooded with His presence and power (demonstrate pouring water to overflowing). The Holy Spirit has come upon us to be effective witnesses for Him, doing the works that He did, John 14:12, followed by speaking a supernatural language. If we want to operate in the gifts of the Holy Spirit, we need to be baptized in the Holy Spirit.

ACTIVATION: The Congregation repeats a prayer for the Baptism of the Holy Spirit.

CHAPTER 6

FELLOWSHIPPING WITH THE HOLY SPIRIT

A. In the midst of the pandemic, the following are still happening:

   1. Many have lost their peace of mind due to fear of catching the coronavirus. As a result, many unbelievers and believers resorted to taking the covid vaccines. Some people had to take the vaccines required by their jobs and some took the vaccines for protection. Then there are those who hesitate taking the vaccines for fear of side-affects.

   2. People all over this nation in the USA and in other nations are protesting against vaccine mandates insisted by the governments, causing the people to lose their freedom of choice and freedom of speech.

3.   Our societies are decaying due to lawlessness, racial issues and government control, using the vaccine mandates. There is an increase of deception everywhere; especially in our government, in support of transgenderism, abortion, homosexual lifestyles, support of Common Core in our public schools, etc. False doctrines have entered in some churches causing some people to fall away from the Christian faith.

4.   Though these things stated above are happening, Jesus Christ says in His Word in Matthew 24:6-10 that, "We are not to be troubled about what is happening for they must come to pass, the end (of the Church Age) is not yet. In other words, don't lose your peace by being upset over what is happening in the world today. For He told us in His Word in Matt. 24 3-10 that these things will happen as signs of His coming. Jesus Christ said in Luke 21:28 (ESV), "When these things begin to take place, straighten up, raise your heads, for your redemption (of your whole body) is drawing near."

It is in these times, in the last of the last days of crisis that we are living in now, that it is important to fellowship or commune with the Holy Spirit; it is a good time to practice the Presence of God. This is why I was inspired to discuss the importance of fellowshipping with the Holy Spirit. It is based on the scripture in 2Corinthians 13:14, "The Grace of the Lord Jesus Christ and the love of God and the Communion of the Holy Spirit be with you all."

The question is, why must we commune with the Holy Spirit?

We have discussed the deity and deeds of the Holy Spirit in chapter 4, however, we can add three more attributes of His deity as a reason we must commune with Him:

1. The Holy Spirit is the very Presence of God who lives in those who accepted Jesus Christ's Spirit in their hearts and whom we fellowship with during our prayer time or devotional time with Him.

2. He is the very voice of God when He speaks to us in our redeemed human spirit- guiding us by the inward witness or intuition, by a still small voice, or an impression in the human spirit- teaching us and showing things to come. As was mentioned in Chapter 4 part B, one of His deeds is for Him to say what He hears the Father God and Jesus Christ say, and The Holy Spirit relays it to Christians within them, when they fellowship with the Holy Spirit during their devotional time with Him.

3. The Holy Spirit is also called "The Spirit of Glory" in 1Peter 4:14. Therefore, we Christians have the Spirit of Glory living within us. His glory abides within us

forever, John 14:16-17. Therefore, we will never fall short of His Glory only fall from His word if we make a mistake of which we must repent immediately of, but we never fall short from His glory. We learn from our mistakes and continue on to be God's son or daughter.

B. How Do We Fellowship With The Holy Spirit?

1. During your devotional time with the Lord for about 15 minutes or more, we are to stir up or kindle the Spirit within us stated in 2Timothy 1:6 and pray in the Spirit or in your spiritual language or in your native language building up your most Holy faith stated in Jude 20.

2. Playing worship songs, praying favorite Psalms. We begin to talk to the Holy Spirit and get Him involved in our daily lives in what we do and consult Him in our decision making.

3. When we talk to the Holy Spirit, we are to sit quiet and expect to hear Him speak to us. Remember, speaking to the Holy Spirit is speaking to God and to Jesus Christ. In John 10:4, in general, Jesus says, "My sheep hear my voice and they follow me."

4. You become more aware of Christ living in you and you in Him. We become one Spirit with the whole Godhead via by the Holy Spirit.

The scripture says in Acts 17:28, "In Him we live and move and have our being," when we practice communing with the Holy Spirit.

C. What Are The Benefits of Fellowshipping With The Holy Spirit or Practicing the Presence of God?

1. When you fellowship with the Holy Spirit as you are praying in the Spirit, you become sensitive to the unction and moves of the Holy Spirit as well as being sensitive to His voice. He connects you more into the spirit realm to the point that you are able to know things to come as well as prophesy.

2. The nine characteristics of the Fruit of the Spirit are developed more within you as you grow spiritually in Christ. We already have Love, Joy, Peace, Longsuffering, Goodness, Kindness, Gentleness or Humility, Faithfulness and Self-control, Galatians 5:22-23. One of the fruits of the Spirit may need to grow more than others that is why God, who began a good work in you, He will complete it.

3. Our faith in God or Jesus Christ is developed when we expect Him to answer our prayers and He answers as we fellowship with the Holy Spirit. He even answers when you pray out His written Word, because His written Word is His will. 1John 5:14-15 (KJV), "This is the confidence or the faith or trust we have in Him that if

we ask anything according to His will, He heareth us and if we know that He hears us, whatsoever we ask, we know that we have the petitions that we desire of Him."

No matter what you hear in the news concerning the coronavirus or Omicron, the new variant, or anything concerning, for example, weather disasters, lawlessness in the streets in all nations, and school shootings that are upsetting, remember, we as Christians must keep our focus on Jesus Christ by practicing His presence or fellowshipping with the Holy Spirit. When we meditate on this, the Holy Spirit will keep us in perfect peace whose mind is stayed on God or Jesus Christ, trusting Him to direct us and protect us during a crisis. When we talk to the Holy Spirit in everything we do and say, we are being consistent in prayer in order to endure these dark days, for God is in it with us to sustain us through it all as we practice His presence that we carry within us everyday.

CHAPTER 7

WHO WE AS CHRISTIANS ARE IN CHRIST VIA THE HOLY SPIRIT

Have you ever heard the expression said by a Christian, "I am just an old sinner saved by grace?" Ephesians 2:8-9 (Amp. Ed.) says, "For it is by free grace (God's unmerited favor) that you are saved (delivered from judgment and made partakers of Christ's salvation) through your faith. And this salvation is not of yourselves (of your own doing. It came not through your own striving) but it is the gift of God.

Not because of works (not the fulfillment of the Law's demands), lest any man should boast. (It is not the result of what anyone can possibly do; so no one can pride himself in it or take glory to himself.)

In the New Living Bible in Ephesians 2:8-9, the scripture more clearly says, "God saved you (past tense) by His special favor when you believed (past tense). And you can't take credit for this, it is a gift from God. Salvation is not a reward for the good things we have done, so none of us can boast about it." Verse 10 says, "For we are God's masterpiece. He has created us anew in Christ Jesus, so that we can do the good things he planned for us long ago."

Such Christians who still think they are sinners saved by grace are thinking sin conscious and believe that they have to recommit their lives to Christ, asking constantly for forgiveness. Such Christians have just made Christ's redemptive work on the cross non-effective in their lives. If we know we made mistakes in life, all we have to do is confess it quickly, ask God for forgiveness and the blood of Jesus Christ erases our sins of the past from our memory. We must forgive ourselves and know that our present and future mistakes are covered by the blood of Jesus, if we quickly repent of them and don't repeat them again but learn through them. You are still a saint and not a sinner because you don't practice sin, according to 1John 3:4-10. In 1John 1:8-9 it seems like God is contradicting Himself, but He is not. I asked the Holy Spirit to explain 1John 1:8-9 that says (NLT), If we say we have no sin, we are only fooling ourselves and refusing to accept the truth (or refusing to admit it). But if we confess our sins to Him, He is faithful and just to forgive us and to cleanse us from every wrong. "The

Holy Spirit revealed the meaning of the scripture saying that this scripture was written to Christians who refuse to admit to doing wrong and to Christians who have backslidden. What the Holy Spirit said to me about this scripture is confirmed in Proverbs 28:13 which says (NLT), "People who cover their sins will not prosper. But if they confess and forsake them, they will receive mercy." In other words, if a Christian knows he did wrong, or if God convicts his or her heart that what was said or done wrong to a recipient was wrong or if a Christian misinterprets a scripture while teaching and does not repent of it or confesses the wrong; or refuses correction by God-perhaps through a prophet, a Christian layman, by a child, or by the Word of God, then he or she is practicing sin. When you confess the mistake you have done or said, it is erased under the blood of Jesus Christ with God's forgiveness, and is forgotten by Him and forgotten by you. You are still a Christian and a child of God that is still growing spiritually. We all learn through our mistakes. We are still saints and not sinners in His Kingdom in that we don't practice sinning. We no longer have the sin nature residing in our human spirit or consciousness according to 1John 3:4-10 (Amp Ed.).

Know this, that the shedding of Christ's blood removed the sin nature within our conscious being or human spirit, but in the process of spiritual growth in Christ, in learning how to live by the Holy Spirit, we are going to make mistakes in life, but we are still saints in God's Kingdom, in that our goal is to please

God. We are to practice walking or living by the Holy Spirit and practice who we are in Christ, which is the new man in us, instead of the old man of worldly thinking that causes us to make many mistakes in life, because we are still living in this body of flesh which is not redeemed yet. It will be redeemed at the time of the rapture of the body of Christ.

So, who are we, Christians in Christ? I will mention a few characteristics of who we are in Christ:

1. Every remnant or true convert Christian is the Temple of the Holy Spirit, 1 Corinthians 6:19. God's Spirit dwells in the redeemed human spirit of a Christian, Proverbs 20:27 which says that the spirit of man is the candle of the Lord. This is why every born again Christian is Holy and has Eternal Life because of the Eternal Holy Spirit living within your human spirit. Therefore, you have the Glory of God living inside you forever. You will never fall from His glory even if you make a mistake. He's in you forever.

2. We are complete in Christ, Colossians 2:9-10 (Amp. Ed.) says, "For in Him (Jesus) the whole fullness of Deity (the Godhead) continues to dwell in bodily form (giving complete expression of the divine nature). And you are in Him made full and having come to fullness of life (in Christ you too are filled with the Godhead - Father, Son and Holy Spirit - and reach full spiritual

stature). And He is the Head of all rule and authority (of every angelic principality and power." We become new creatures in that we are the reflection of Christ's Spirit living in us the hope of glory, Galatians 2:20. Therefore, the kingdom of God resides in us, because of our connection with the Spirit of Christ, who is the Holy Spirit, Luke 17:21 (KJV). In His Kingdom there is healing and all that we need, therefore, let us speak it forth into existence, expecting it to happen presently or in due season, using the faith God gave us as what we expect is revealed to us. That is, if we see in the spirit or we imagine that we have what we say, it will eventually manifest. That takes practice.

3. You are a chosen generation, a royal Priesthood. A holy nation, 1 Peter 2:9. You are God's very own possession. As a result, you show others the goodness of God, for He Called you out of darkness into His marvelous light.

4. We have become ambassadors for Jesus Christ, 2Corinthians 5:20. We are to do the work of reconciliation. Jesus said, the works that He did we can do too and even greater works. John 14:12. This includes doing the Great Commission stated in Mark 16:15-18 (NLT) saying, "Go into all the world and preach (or share) the gospel (or the good news about the life of Jesus, His death, burial and resurrection, as well as about the Kingdom of God). Anyone who

believes and is baptized shall be saved. Anyone who refuses to believe will be condemned. And these signs will accompany those who believe: They will cast out demons in my name, they will speak in new languages; they will be able to handle snakes with safety; if they drink anything poisonous, it won't hurt them; they will be able to place their hands on the sick and heal them (or they shall recover)."

5. We are no longer sinners saved by grace, but saints because of the redemptive work Jesus did on the cross to deliver us from the sin nature whose blood has covered all of our sins once and for all once we repent of them. We cannot be a sinner and a saint at the same time. You are either a saint or a sinner. If you're a sinner you are still practicing sin. You are in the family of the devil, but if you practice righteousness with the help of the Holy Spirit, you have the divine seed of God's divine nature. Read 1John 3:4-10, again. Even if you make a mistake, repenting of it is part of God cleansing you. You have not fallen from His glory because Jesus said, He will never leave you nor forsake you, nor will you be snatched from the Father's hand. You may fall from His word when you make a mistake, but never His glory or the Holy Spirit (1Peter 4:14, Holy Spirit is the Spirit of Glory) who abides within you forever, John 14:17. We never fall short of His glory.

I end with this encouraging message I received from Cal Pierce's Healing Ministry on Facebook: "Who you are carries the power, what you say directs the power"; that is within you. Min. Pierce also said, "If God is in you and you want a move of God, start movin'." In other words, start living by the God consciousness of who you are in Christ and live by the Holy Spirit, doing what He calls you to do; and not by the sin consciousness condemning yourself over every mistake you make. Jesus said, I have come that you may have life, and have life more abundantly. That is, life lived more abundantly is manifested by us being led by the dictates of the Holy Spirit, who determines us as a new creature in Christ and having the mind of Christ. Let no one- no pastor, no leader, no family member, no friend -deter you from knowing who you are in Christ. In fact, they should help build you up and encourage you to be who you are in Christ and disciple you to grow spiritually as to who you are in Christ by the Word of God. Knowing who you are in Christ would help a Christian brother or sister to overcome their feelings of depression, condemnation, and low self-esteem.

THE END

OTHER BOOKS OF THE AUTHOR

The books below can be purchased at Amazon.com and
Barnes and Nobles.com.

Eschatology Book:

This book indicates the signs of events happening
today and signs that will happen in the near future
that tell that the coming of Jesus Christ is near at
the door. The book includes events that will occur
during the Rapture, the Great Tribulation, The
Millennial Age and the Perfect Age. Each Age is
defined and its events discussed.

Simple Prophecy Handbook:

This prophetic handbook is for interested readers
who are either called into the prophetic ministry
or who are interested in knowing about the
prophetic in general. This book has activation
exercises to help the reader to identify the various
methods of prophecy operating in him or her and
how to identify God's voice from within and by
His written Word in the Bible.

Handbook For Understanding Your Dreams And Interpreting Them:

This book is for the reader who interested in
understanding their dreams and visions. He or she
will learn the definitions of a dream, vision and
Trances and how to interpret them. The reader
will learn the meanings of symbols in a dream and
vision, the meaning of colors, numbers and various
categories of dreams. How to identify ways God
speaks; especially, through dreams and visions.

www.ingramcontent.com/pod-product-compliance
Lightning Source LLC
Chambersburg PA
CBHW051251120626
46547CB00014B/1888